the
Price
of
Free Land

by TREVA ADAMS STRAIT

J. B. Lippincott   New York

U.S. Library of Congress Cataloging in Publication Data

Strait, Treva Adams, birth date
    The price of free land.

    SUMMARY: The author relates her family's experiences
as homesteaders in western Nebraska in 1914.
        1. Strait, Treva Adams, birth date—Juvenile literature.
2. Nebraska—Biography—Juvenile literature.   3. Frontier
and pioneer life—Nebraska—Juvenile literature.   4. Nebraska—
History—Juvenile literature.   5. Pioneers—Nebraska—Biography—
Juvenile literature.   [1. Frontier and pioneer life.   2. Nebraska—
History]   I. Title.
F666.S88   978.2'03'0924 [B]   78-24287
ISBN-0-397-31836-7   ISBN-0-397-31883-9 (LB)

In loving memory
of
my parents,
Merlan and Edna Adams

Contents

*Eight pages of pictures
appear between pages 42 and 51.*

Foreword

IN 1914, when I was five years old, we homesteaded in western Nebraska twelve miles north of Scottsbluff. The total expense for the 320 acres my parents came to own was twenty-four dollars, but the hardships we endured carried no price tag.

Although this book covers the time when I was a child, the incidents in it, and even some of the conversations, are very vivid to me. All the people in the book are real, but I have changed some of their names.

I wish to thank Mr. Donald D. Snoddy, assistant state archivist at the Nebraska State Historical Society in Lincoln, who sent me much-needed information to authenticate my book. A copy of the records concerning the homestead from the National Archives in Washington, D.C., was invaluable.

the Land

ON THE THIRD SUNDAY in May, 1914, we saw for the first time the land that was to become our home. I was almost five years old. My brother, Howard, was seven, and Dorothy, the baby, was only six months old.

Papa pulled on the mare's reins. "Whoa, Betsy." The buggy stopped in the midst of a large flock of sheep. The prairie around us was a carpet of green tufted with smoke-gray sagebrush.

"Look at this! Just look at this! And it's going to be *ours*," Papa said as he jumped down from the buggy. He stretched his arms wide.

"My, you sound confident," said Mamma. "But we have to remember, thirteen other people filed for this same piece of land." She surveyed the vast area from the high buggy seat. "Where would we build the house?"

Papa didn't answer her. He was dreaming his own dreams. "Isn't it beautiful? We'll plant trees so we can have shade and listen to the birds sing. I've missed the trees since we came to western Nebraska."

"All I see are sheep, cattle, grass, hills, and that big lake," said Mamma. "I can't see one house. That means we'll have no close neighbors."

Howard stood up in the buggy. "Look, Mamma, there's a house on the other side of the lake."

"You're right. And if I were a bird I'd fly across the lake to see who lives there. It must be over a mile."

The lake was to the north of us. To the east the prairie looked as though it extended forever. To the west were rolling hills, and on the south more low hills, topped by two high, cream-colored clay ones of irregular shape.

Mamma was looking down at the grass, first on one side of the buggy and then on the other. "What are you looking for, Mamma?" I asked.

"I was wondering if there could be rattlesnakes here."

Papa said, "I haven't seen any, but I'm sure there are. Everyone will have to be careful. It would take at least two hours for a doctor to get here from Scottsbluff."

"Can I have a pony when we live here?" Howard asked. "With a pony I can watch the cows for you."

"We'll see. First we'll have to make enough money to buy the cows," Papa said as he let a handful of fine earth sift through his fingers. "This land will raise the best potatoes western Nebraska has ever seen. We'll sell enough of them to buy some cattle."

Mamma looked at the prairie again. "I wonder where we'll build our house," she said softly.

"When are we coming to live here, Papa?" Howard asked.

Papa walked over to rub Betsy on the nose. "The settlement date, as the government calls it, is exactly three months from today. We'll be here bright and early on August 17. Over a million settlers have been given free land since President

Lincoln signed the Homestead Act, and now we'll join them."

Howard had an idea. "Why can't we come a day early? Then we'd be ahead of everyone else. You said the first one who drives all the stakes will get the land."

"We have to follow the rules. The General Land Office in Washington, D.C., wrote a letter. It says that if anyone goes on the land before nine o'clock on August 17, he will be considered a trespasser and will lose all right to the land."

"We sure don't want that to happen," Mamma said. "Your father and I have been married nine years and we've moved twenty-three times. We're ready to settle down."

"While we're here today, I want to locate the corners of the land," Papa said as he climbed back into the buggy. "They told me in the General Land Office that the surveyors put steel markers in plain sight."

"I thought you said we'd be trespassers," Howard reminded him as we began to bump over the rough ground.

"The letter also said we could go over the land to examine it, and that's what we're doing today. We'll drive up to that barbed wire fence. I know one of the markers is there. We'll follow the fence east for a quarter of a mile, and we should find another marker."

When we reached the first marker, Papa tied a rag on the rim of the buggy wheel and told us to count how many times the wheel went around. When the rag had hit the ground 110 times, he figured, we'd have gone a quarter of a mile. "If we don't make too many mistakes counting," he said, "we should find all the markers."

"Why do we have to find all of them?" Howard asked.

"I have to drive a stake beside each marker when I race to get this land," said Papa.

Mamma, Papa, and Howard counted out loud as we

bumped over the prairie. Dorothy slept in Mamma's arms.

When we reached the foot of a big butte, Papa stopped Betsy. "Everyone out. I'll unloosen Betsy's bit so she can enjoy some of this good grass."

The base of the hill looked like the claws of a huge lion, because rain and snow had washed gullies about every twenty or thirty feet. Cottontails looked at me with their big round eyes, and I wanted to catch one. I ran, climbed, and crawled as fast as I could after them, but the little animals kept just a few feet ahead of me. When I looked back, I was high above my family.

"Don't you fall," Mamma called up to me. "Watch out for snakes. Be careful of your dress."

After a while, Papa called us back. "We've only found two markers. We'd better get going."

It took a long time to find all the markers. On the way home, Papa said, "It'll be easier next time. I'll come several times this summer so I'll know right where they are on the day of the run."

He added, "Even though fourteen people have filed for this piece of land, I feel I have the inside track. I was the one who requested that this area be surveyed. . . . Fourteen people! It should be quite a race."

Mamma said, "Do you suppose someday they'll tell about it in the Nebraska history books? No one has raced for land since the Oklahoma Panhandle was settled."

"When was that?" Howard asked.

"Well, I was just a little boy then," said Papa. "I'm thirty-one now. I must have been about ten, so that would be about twenty years ago. My grandfather was in that race. He was lucky, and I think we'll be lucky, too."

Waiting for August 17

PAPA HAD BEGUN WORK for the local irrigation district in April, 1914. He earned thirty cents an hour working as a ditch rider. Seven days a week he rode through the area turning the irrigation water on and off as the farmers requested. He also had to record the amount of water that flowed onto the land.

During the summer of 1914 we lived in a small house at an abandoned construction camp. We moved there from Scottsbluff the last of May. The only thing I really liked about our temporary home was my playhouse. It was on the top of a platform about ten feet above the ground. The playhouse was five feet square, with a wooden floor and roof, and screening for walls. There was a ladder leading up to it. Papa put the steps on the ladder closer together so I could get up there by myself.

Mamma explained, "When a lot of men lived here, this was a meat house. When they butchered a cow or a pig they hung it here. It was high enough to be away from dogs and cats, and the screen kept out the flies."

From my playhouse I could watch the road. Once in a while a car went by, but mostly I saw buggies and farm wagons.

One day I watched a wagon approach from the south. It was loaded with small boxes and crates. A man wearing a straw hat with a torn rim sat on the seat driving the team. When he got right in front of our house, a wheel hit a chughole in the road and the endgate of the wagon shook loose. I saw something fall out.

I came down my ladder as fast as I could, and Mamma and Howard came running. The horses stopped and the driver climbed down.

"I was taking this to a country store in Sioux County," he said, "but it looks as though you folks will have some free Christmas candy." He lifted the empty cardboard box. There on the ground was hard candy of all colors and shapes.

"Run get some pails," Mamma said.

The three of us filled two milk pails while the driver readjusted the endgate, wired it shut, and drove away.

When Papa got home, I ran to meet him. "You won't never have to buy me any more candy!" I announced. "A man just put some in the road for us."

The only other children we saw that summer were a boy and girl who lived about a quarter of a mile from us. We saw them every day when we went to get the Omaha *Daily News* that the rural carrier left in our mailbox. We tried to talk to them, but they never said anything. Often they followed us back toward our house.

One evening Howard told Papa about them. "They can't talk," he said.

Papa said, "They don't understand English. They just came from Russia. Their parents were hired to work in the beet fields."

"Won't they *ever* be able to talk?" I asked.

"Oh, they talk to their parents in Russian. This fall they'll go to school and learn English."

Papa told us he had known other immigrants.

"When I was fifteen years old, I went to the harvest fields in North and South Dakota. I met many young men from Europe who spoke very little English."

"You mean you started working when you were fifteen?" Howard said. "And you never went to school anymore?"

"No, not after I finished the ninth grade. But wherever I worked, I listened to instructions, and read newspapers and magazines and books. I guess you'd call me a self-educated man."

"Is that why we get the newspaper every day?" I asked. "So you'll always be smart?"

"I suppose you might say that. Your mother and I lived near Omaha, so we like to know what's happening there. The paper also keeps us informed about the rest of our country and the world."

"Will we get the paper when we move to the homestead?"

"Of course. We'll just move our mailbox to the main road nearest our new home."

All of us were happy when July was gone. August was hotter and drier, but every day we were getting closer to the seventeenth.

the Great Day

SOON AFTER PAPA RETURNED from work on Sunday, August 16, our friend Mr. Harding and his son Charley drove into the yard with a hayrack. The men began loading our belongings.

"Do you suppose you and Charley could start putting up our tents while I'm driving the stakes tomorrow?" Papa asked Mr. Harding. "I understand that it's important to get these things done quickly. Especially if more than one person claims the land at the end of the three years."

"Do you know where you want the tents to go?" Mr. Harding asked.

"Each of the fourteen claimants was given a certain place to establish a home. We've been assigned the northwest corner."

"Will everyone be bringing a house along, the way you folks are?"

"I really don't know. The law says we have six months to establish a home and cultivate part of the land. Maybe some will just drive their stakes tomorrow."

Soon the hayrack was piled high with tents, boxes,

Mamma's precious clocks, furniture, pieces of tin, boards of various lengths, and a crate that would hold our chickens.

We stayed the night with the Hardings. The next morning, after a hurried breakfast, we were ready to go. Papa rode Betsy, and Mamma, Howard, and I climbed on the hayrack with Mr. Harding and Charley. Mamma sat in the little rocker with Dorothy on her lap. Howard found a place on the edge of the hayrack and let his legs hang over. I sat in Papa's big rocking chair as we drove the two miles to the homestead.

When we drew near the homestead, we could see many people walking around. "Who are all those men?" Howard asked.

Papa said, "Well, each settler must have a lawyer, a timekeeper, and a starter. And some of those people could be friends or just sightseers."

A man strode toward us. "Good morning, Merlan," he said to Papa. "All of us timekeepers met at eight this morning to set our watches at exactly the same time."

Our starter said, "My gun is cocked, ready for action."

Our lawyer, Mr. Scott, was there, too. "Everything's in order, as far as I can see. We just have to wait until nine o'clock."

Each claimant was to start the race from the place that had been assigned as his homesite. After the race started, claimants could go to the right or the left around the land, whichever they preferred. Before we got off the hayrack, Howard and I took a long look at the groups of people ranged along the borders of the homestead. Then we climbed down, and Mr. Harding and Charley drove the horses to the very edge of the coveted land.

"Don't you put your foot over there or you'll be a trespasser," Howard warned me. "Then the land won't be ours."

Papa got off Betsy. From the saddlebag he took a hammer and one of the stakes, a two-foot piece of wood with one end shaped to a point.

Our starter climbed up on Mr. Harding's hayrack so everyone could see him. "Adams, are you ready?" he yelled.

"Yeah!"

"Here goes!" the starter yelled, and, when he received the signal from the timekeeper, he fired his revolver into the air.

Papa stepped onto the northwest corner of the land. He drove the first stake with three hard hammer blows.

"Hurrah!" the crowd cheered.

"Good luck!" Mamma called as Papa leapt onto Betsy's back. The two of them sped away.

We saw Papa pull on Betsy's reins as he approached the southwest corner. He jumped off and drove the second stake. Betsy was ready to go as soon as Papa grasped the dangling reins. She scarcely let him get settled in the saddle before she was off at a fast gallop.

Mr. Harding and Charley had driven the hayrack onto the land as soon as the starters fired their guns. Soon Mr. Harding walked toward us carrying a rocking chair. "Mrs. Adams, you'd better sit down. I know that baby is heavy. This is going to be a long day, and you'd better try to relax a little. Sit here in the shade of the hayrack."

"Thank you so much," said Mamma.

"It must be over 100 degrees," he said as he set the rocker down.

"Here he comes! Here he comes!" I yelled at the top of my voice. Some of the people clapped their hands, while others threw their hats into the air and cheered. It had taken Papa half an hour to drive the stakes.

Papa jumped from Betsy's back and patted her lathered shoulder. "Good girl. We did it!"

Mr. Scott stepped forward. "It looks good. I believe you're the first one to get all the stakes driven. In fact, I've seen some people going past here who appear to be lost. They're probably still trying to find the corners."

"How many stakes have been driven here besides mine?" Papa asked.

"At this corner? Only two others so far."

Papa looked at the three stakes thoughtfully and then said, "I didn't see many people while I was making the rounds. Some fellows were going in the opposite direction. I didn't recognize any of them. . . . I'm beginning to wonder if all fourteen applicants are racing today. Maybe some changed their minds after they filed at the land office."

Mr. Scott said, "We'll probably never know. I should have counted how many timekeepers showed up at eight this morning, but I didn't think of it."

Papa and Mr. Harding unloaded our water barrel from the hayrack, and Mamma found the box that held the glasses. We all lined up and she filled our glasses from the big dipper.

Then the men got to work setting up our tents. First they drove four-foot tent stakes into the hard ground. Then, with lumber, they built triangular frames to hold up the roofs of our new home.

There were two tents—a big one that we'd live in, and a small one for the kitchen and storage. There were metal rings at the bottoms of the tents, and Papa laced them with rope. The sides of each tent could be rolled up to the tops of the stakes and fastened there, to let in light and air; but when the sides were down and the ropes tied fast to the stakes, our home would be snug and secure.

Papa cut a hole in each tent where the sides touched, so we could go from one to the other. Then Charley and his father helped Papa level the ground inside the tents.

Neither of the tents had been made with doorways. You were supposed to go in and out by ducking under the sides. But Mr. Harding made us a real doorway—he cut another hole in the smaller tent, framed it with boards, and hung a screen door we had brought with us.

Mamma carefully covered the ground inside the tents with burlap sacks that she had ripped open and washed. She told Howard and me to make nests for the chickens and let them out of their coop. We took an empty orange crate and filled it with dry grass. The dozen Buff Orphington hens came out of their coop holding their wings out stiffly at their sides and looking nervously about them.

"They're hot, Mamma," said Howard. "Can we give them a drink?"

"We have to save the water in the barrel for drinking and cooking. Do you suppose you two could go to the lake for water? You'll have to watch for snakes. We'll eat as soon as you get back."

Each of us took an empty five-pound syrup pail and started on our journey. The water in the lake was very low, and we had to walk over half a mile before we could fill our pails.

When we got back, Howard poured water into a coffee can for the hens. I set my pail down and started for the tent, and nearly stepped on an egg. There was another close by, and soon Howard found five more. Mamma fried the eggs and called us to the table. She had made sandwiches with her good home-baked bread, and had opened a jar of peaches. We ate at the dining table inside the tent, because it was too hot to eat outdoors. My, I was hungry. It had been a very long morning.

When we had finished eating, Papa said, "Now I'd better start digging a cellar. I wouldn't trust this tent in a big storm."

"I'll take a chance on the storm for a few days," Mamma said in a determined voice. "We need a toilet."

Papa didn't argue with her. "It's a good thing I brought lumber along."

"Why don't you make one low seat for Dorothy? She'll soon be big enough to use it."

Papa and Howard went outside, and Mamma spent the afternoon unpacking boxes. She put the dishes and silverware in the glass-fronted cupboard. Her two old clocks were set safely on top.

Later that afternoon, Howard came in to announce, "The backhouse is done. Papa wants you to see it."

"Our backhouse is fancier than our home—it has a wooden floor," Papa said. "We'd better remember to keep the door shut. That should keep out the snakes."

We ate our evening meal outdoors at an old table that Mamma had covered with bright yellow oilcloth. As she sat down, she said, "I'm almost too tired to eat."

"We'll all be happy to see this day come to a close," said Papa as he slumped into his chair. "After supper I'll take Betsy to the lake for a drink, and I'll have a swim."

"Would you bring a pail of water so I can wash the dishes?"

Mamma helped us children get to bed and listened to our prayers. We slept in folding cots that would be stored behind Mamma's and Papa's bed in the daytime.

Before they went to bed, Mamma and Papa lowered the sides of the tents and fastened them securely. They didn't want any unwelcome callers to disturb our sleep.

Getting Settled

EARLY THE NEXT MORNING, Papa went off to his job riding ditch. He left before we children awoke.

Mamma rolled up the straight sides of the larger tent. When the roll reached the top of the tent stakes, she tied it in place. This kept our home cool and let natural light come in.

About noon, we saw two men with a wagonload of lumber. They were headed toward the southwest corner of the homestead. Close behind them was a young couple in a polished black buggy drawn by a team of matched grays.

Mamma said, "They must be some of the people who drove stakes yesterday."

"Will they get our land?" Howard asked.

"I hope not. But we'll just have to wait and see. If we and they are still living here three years from now, the government will decide who owns the land. In the meantime, we'll have close neighbors, and that will be fine."

Howard and I spent the afternoon watching the men work.

Before they left, a foundation of heavy timbers had been placed in a rectangle. Then two-by-fours were nailed upright, two feet apart, to form the framework of a small house.

That evening, Mamma told Papa about the new neighbors. "How many people do you suppose will finally settle with us?"

"Since there's only three stakes at this corner," said Papa, "that must indicate that just three of the fourteen will lay claim."

"I wonder where the third person will settle," Mamma said.

"We'll just have to wait and see," Papa said. "If there's going to be a contest, I'm glad we got settled first. Even if it's only in a tent."

Washday

PAPA BUILT A SLED from boards nailed on smooth runners so he and Betsy could bring well water from the abandoned construction camp where we'd been living. The sled was large enough to carry two ten-gallon milk cans. The well water he brought home each evening was used only for cooking and drinking. All the water for cleaning, for Dorothy's bath, for the hens, and for washing faces and hands was brought from the lake in the boiler on our little wagon. Fetching water was a daily chore for Howard and me.

"You'd better go now," Mamma would say right after breakfast. "It's going to get very hot. Each of you take your pail. Don't play in the water, just fill the boiler and come right home. I can't see you when you're down at the lake, and I'll worry if you're gone too long."

The lake was our bathtub. Howard and I spent many hours wading and swimming. Papa took a swim every evening. Mamma generally took her bath in the washtub at home. Papa laughed. "You're afraid a cow might look at you," he would tease her.

Before Mamma could wash our clothes, she needed a clothesline and a way to heat wash water. For the clothesline, Papa dug two holes and then nailed two-by-two boards across the tops of two long posts. When the posts were firmly set in the holes, he stretched two lines of smooth baling wire between the extended crosspieces.

We all went to the lake to watch Papa build the fireplace. Howard helped him find enough large flat stones to make a U-shaped wall about two feet high. The top stones were level enough to support the boiler.

Howard and I collected pine and cedar driftwood at the edge of the lake. Papa laid a bed of dry weeds in the fireplace. Then he put the driftwood pieces on top. "When this is lighted, you'll have hot water in short order," he said to Mamma. "Just keep putting fresh wood on the fire as it burns."

The next morning, Mamma loaded the soiled laundry into the boiler, which was already on our wagon. She put Dorothy in the baby buggy and tied the galvanized tub and a large enamel bucket to the front of the buggy. The washboard and a bar of homemade soap lay at Dorothy's feet.

When we reached the fireplace, Mamma lighted the fire. She took the clothes out of the boiler and sorted them into piles on the ground. "You children bring water in your pails to fill the boiler half full," she said.

When the water was very hot, Mamma used a paring knife to shave pieces of soap into it. With an old broom handle that we called a clothes stick she stirred the water until the soap had dissolved. Then she put in the white clothes. While they boiled, she filled the galvanized tub half full of water. After the clothes had boiled for ten minutes, she lifted them into the enamel bucket with the clothes stick and then dumped them into the tub. She carefully inspected each article for dirty spots. When she found one, she rubbed soap on the area, then scrubbed it firmly on the washboard.

After the white clothes were washed, she washed the colored clothes, and last of all Papa's work clothes and Howard's overalls. She dipped the hot water out of the boiler with the bucket. Then she filled the boiler again and rinsed the clothes. While Mamma was busy washing, Howard and I piled driftwood for the fireplace.

After a long and tiring morning, the washing was done. We loaded the clean clothes onto the wagon and started home. Howard pulled the wagon, and Mamma pushed Dorothy in her buggy. When we were about halfway home, I tapped Howard's arm. "I touched you last!" I crowed, and skipped away.

Howard tried to reach me with his free hand to return the tag. Somehow he upset the wagon, and all the laundry came tumbling out onto the dry grass and earth.

"Now see what you've done!" Mamma scolded. She grabbed each of us in turn and spanked us.

We reloaded the clothes and returned to the lake shore. Every piece had to be rinsed all over again. It was nearly the middle of the afternoon before the clothes were hung to dry.

As we ate a very late meal, Mamma said, "Work while you work, play while you play."

I'd heard her say that before, but this time I listened.

the Storm Cellar

ONE DAY, our neighbors stopped by to introduce themselves. They were Kenneth and Mary Patterson.

"I'm glad to meet you," Mamma said. "It makes me feel better to have close neighbors. I've lived most of my life in the city. I like to have people around."

"Kenneth thinks we should try to own some land," Mrs. Patterson said, "and this is practically free. But I really don't like the idea at all. I'd rather live in town. We'll be spending part of each week there."

"You'll be here only part of the time?" Mamma asked.

"We have to stay here four nights of each week, if we are to claim that we have established a home. I sure couldn't stay here all the time like you do."

"This is our home," Mamma said, as she pushed Dorothy's buggy back and forth. "I'm glad you stopped to say hello. It gets pretty lonely here."

From then on, the Pattersons stopped a few minutes to chat whenever they were going by.

A couple of evenings after we'd settled on the homestead, Papa said, "I must get started on that cellar. We never know when there'll be a big storm."

He rose and swung Dorothy astride his shoulders. He strolled across the prairie a few yards with all of us following. "We'll put it over here. That will make it about twenty feet east of where we'll build our house."

"How big will it be?" Howard asked.

"It has to be deep enough for me to stand erect in, and big enough for all of us to get into in case of a tornado or a bad windstorm."

"And big enough for shelves to store a lot of things that are now piled in the kitchen," Mamma added.

"I'll make it about ten by twelve feet, and seven feet deep. If I make it too big I'll never get it dug."

Papa stepped off the outline of the cellar, and Howard laid two-by-fours along the outline to show its shape. "We'll put the opening toward the tent," Papa said, and marked the location of the steps with his shovel.

Howard helped Papa start removing the prairie grass and the top layer of soil from the area inside the two-by-fours. Papa cut the sod loose and Howard carried it away.

"That's enough for tonight," Papa said after a while. He patted Howard's shoulder. "That's a good beginning."

Each evening after supper, Papa and Howard worked on the cellar, and the hole grew deeper and wider. To be sure the sides would be straight up and down, they made a plumb line. One end of a six-foot length of string was fastened to a two-by-four at the edge of the cellar wall. Papa tied a screwdriver to the other end to make it taut. When the string hung from the two-by-four, it was plumb—straight up and down.

It took about a week to finish the digging. Then Papa covered the hole with planks and shoveled dirt over them. The dirt on top was piled into a dome shape, so that water would run off when it rained. Papa made a ventilation hole in the center and ran a short length of stovepipe through it. Finally, he nailed twelve-inch boards together to make the door that covered the entrance.

"We'll feel much safer now," Papa said as he sat in his rocker admiring the first permanent structure on the homestead. "We'll put a kerosene lantern and a box of matches on the top shelf so they will be there in case we need them. I'll try to get the shelves made before the week is over."

When the four shelves were finished, Mamma carried all the glass jars that were filled with fruit to the cellar. Papa had bought milk and butter from a nearby farmer, and Mamma put them in the cellar too. She said, "We'll keep the vegetables in one corner. . . . I must remember to save enough room for all of us to get in here if necessary. I sure hope that never happens."

the Tornado

DRIED COW DROPPINGS, which we called cow chips, made a quick, hot, clean fire. "One good thing about burning chips," Mamma told Papa one evening, "is that the kitchen cools as soon as I'm through cooking. But it seems as though all I do is fill the stove. It takes about three sacks each day to heat the water and cook the meals."

It was a daily chore to find a place where the cattle had ranged at least a week before. Even in hot weather it took that long for the chips to dry enough so they could be used for fuel. The dry chips were about six inches in diameter, grayish white, and not easily broken.

When we went to look for chips, Dorothy sat high in her buggy with three gunnysacks folded neatly beneath her. Mamma pushed the buggy slowly over the rough prairie so the wheels wouldn't come loose. Howard and I ran ahead to look for chips.

When the sacks were filled, we loaded them into the buggy.

Howard pushed it home, and Mamma carried Dorothy. I was careful not to bother Howard, because I remembered what had happened on washday.

It was the last Friday in August when the tornado came. As Mamma lifted the third sack of chips into the buggy, we saw a funnel-shaped cloud in the west. It was moving rapidly toward us, its tail on the ground.

"A tornado!" Mamma gasped. "Howard, Treva, run!" She pulled up her long skirt and began to run, carrying Dorothy.

The atmosphere was very still. It was eerie—we felt as though there was no air to breathe. As we ran for the tents, the wind began to blow. Soon it was so strong we were fighting for each step.

Mamma took Dorothy into the cellar. Then we three unrolled the sides of the tents and tied them down firmly as the dust whirled about us.

As I started toward the cellar, the wind swept me off my feet, but Howard helped me up. We climbed down into the cellar. The open door of the cellar lay flat on the ground, and when Mamma tried to lift it, it wouldn't budge. The wind held it firmly in place. "Dear God, give me strength," she prayed. Twice the wind jerked the door from her grasp, but the third time, with a mighty tug, she pulled it up. Quickly she stepped inside on the stairs and pulled the door down over the opening.

We all sat silently on the floor of the cellar, listening to the howl of the wind and the sound of loose objects rolling by outside. Through the ventilation hole we could see the clouds tumbling about.

"Mamma, will the wind take the tents?" I whispered.

"I don't know," she answered softly and slowly.

As suddenly as the storm had come, it was gone. We could hear nothing. The tiny spot of sky we could see through the hole was blue again.

"It's over," Mamma said as she rose to her feet. "Your father was right when he decided we needed a storm cellar." She went up the stairs and lifted the door. Howard followed, carrying Dorothy, and I came last.

"It's here! It's still here! Thank you, God," Mamma said as she looked at our home. Her eyes were filled with tears.

"And we've still got the backhouse," said Howard. "But where's my wagon? Mamma, look at the woodpile! It's scattered all over. And the boiler is way over there."

Four of the hens were sitting near the boiler. Two had broken legs. The other two were dead. We put all four into the boiler and carried them home.

Mamma stepped on the heads of the two dead hens one at a time. She gave a quick jerk and the blood flowed freely as the heads came off.

"As long as the blood hasn't set, they'll be all right to eat," she told us. "I'll start the fire and get some water hot right away so we can pluck them. Now let's see those other hens."

"Can you fix their legs like a doctor?" Howard asked.

"I'll try."

She fastened a little stick to each broken leg with a narrow strip of cloth. "We'll have to bring them their water and feed until their legs mend."

We were watching them try to move about when Howard exclaimed, "Mamma, look! The Pattersons' house is gone!"

Howard was right. The small frame house was gone. Its pieces were scattered over the prairie.

"And this is their day to come back from town," said

Mamma. "What a terrible sight to come back to! And these tents stood, while a frame house was torn apart. I just can't understand it."

Everything in our tents was gray with dust. After Mamma started the fire, we took up the sacks that covered the floor and carried them outdoors. We shook each one and carefully relaid it. Mamma hung her big bedspread on the clothesline and beat it with the broom. I took a cloth and pushed the dust from the chairs and table into a bucket. Mamma removed the rest of the dust with a damp cloth.

"Tomorrow I'll have to take all the dishes from the china cupboard and wash them," she said. "All we can do today is get this place clean enough for us to sleep in."

About four o'clock the Pattersons' buggy stopped near our tents. Mamma told them about the storm.

"We lived here less than two weeks. Now we're wiped out," Kenneth Patterson said. He turned to his wife. "It looks as though your wish has come true."

"I didn't like it here, but I didn't want it to end like this," she said. "You worked so hard to build our little house."

"Thank God we weren't here today," he said. He put a comforting arm around her as they drove on toward the place where their house had been.

Later the Pattersons stopped at our tents again. They were on their way back to town. "For some unknown reason I've had a feeling this wasn't going to be our home," said Kenneth. "This settled it."

"Then you aren't going to rebuild?" Mamma asked.

"Nope. The homestead is all yours as far as we're concerned. We're going back to Lincoln, where Mary's parents live."

"Mrs. Adams, I hate to say good-bye to you. You're a

33

wonderful person. I wish I had your optimism," Mary said as she reached over the side of the buggy to shake Mamma's hand.

"I'll miss you so much. You were wonderful neighbors," Mamma said, and wiped her eyes.

It was nearly six before we saw Papa and Betsy coming from work. Howard and I ran to meet him and tell him about the tornado.

"I hear it was quite a day," Papa said to Mamma when we all got home.

Mamma smiled as she said, "I've decided that if we can live through a tornado, we can live through anything."

"From what the children have told me, I've decided you're stronger than a tornado," said Papa.

A Trip to Town

WHEN PAPA RETURNED HOME the last evening in August, he reported that school would begin the following Monday.

"Howard needs shoes and we need groceries," Mamma said, "so you two had better go to town Saturday. It's been a month since you went last."

"I'll get someone to take my place on the ditch. And there's a cart I sometimes use when I ride the ditch; I'll bring it home with me Friday evening, and we'll go to town in it."

"Can I go too?" I asked.

"No, not this time. You'll have to take care of Mamma and Dorothy. But I'll bring you something."

Saturday morning Mamma had a list ready. She placed a galvanized can with a screw lid in the cart. "We'll be using the lamps more now that the days are getting shorter," she said, "so you'd better get five gallons of coal oil. Be sure to keep it away from the groceries."

Papa and Howard left soon after breakfast. I helped Mamma and played with Dorothy. It was a very long day for me.

35

Papa and Howard returned just before dark. I ran out to greet them. Before I could ask for my surprise, Howard announced, "Betsy ran away."

"What do you mean?" Mamma asked.

"Lucky for us a farmer caught her after she left us sitting in the road down by the cemetery," Papa said as he jumped down from the cart.

"I don't understand," Mamma complained.

Papa and Howard explained, talking in turn. When Papa paid for the groceries, Cecil, the grocery store owner, gave him six sticks of licorice for Howard. Cecil put them in a red and white striped bag. Then Papa and Howard started home.

"After I ate the licorice, I blew up the bag and popped it," said Howard.

"Betsy bolted as though she'd been hit with a club," said Papa. "I didn't have a tight hold on the reins, so they just slid through my fingers. We sailed off the seat backwards quicker than I can tell about it. I hit the ground so hard it jarred my teeth. I didn't know which end of me hurt the worst. Howard jumped up right away, so I knew he was all right. He thought if we ran fast enough we could catch Betsy, but I knew better."

"Bob Jones caught her," Howard said. "He tied her to his front gate."

"Bob was just ready to milk the cows in the corral when he saw her coming down the road," Papa went on. "He said she was walking at a steady pace, but he had no trouble stopping her."

"What happened to the groceries?"

"Nothing, thank goodness. Lucky for us the coal oil didn't spill. And, Treva, I got home with your surprise." He handed me a small box.

"Ribbons! Two red ones! Thank you, Papa."

Papa had brought Dorothy a rubber doll that made a squeaky sound when we pressed on her stomach. "Mamma, what did Papa bring you?" I asked.

"I don't know yet. I'll look at the groceries first."

She pushed aside the blue and white gingham curtain at the front of the pantry cupboard. The cupboard was made of orange crates stacked on end, one above another. Mamma put the bags of white navy beans, prunes, dried apples, dried peaches, and raisins on the top shelves. Canned milk filled one shelf; two ten-pound pails of lard were stored in the bottom. Papa dumped the twenty-five-pound sack of flour into the flour bin in the kitchen cabinet. The spices were put on the narrow shelves at the top of the cabinet. Mamma filled the big glass jar that sat on her work space with white sugar. Carrots and turnips would go into a box of sand in the cellar.

Mamma's surprise was two yards of bright pink calico for an apron. "I figured it would give this place some extra color," Papa said.

It took a long time to eat supper that night, because Papa and Howard entertained us with more stories about the day's experiences.

"You should have seen the cars that went past us," said Howard. "Four of them were Fords and one was a Dodge. They sure went fast."

Papa said, "They left us in the dust. I suppose they were going thirty miles an hour. Someday I sure hope to own a Dodge. I'd never want a Ford. The back end jumps around too much. I couldn't watch the front end and the back end at the same time. A Dodge is heavier."

Howard put in, "You should see the Edwards' house! They don't have to pump water anymore. They just turn the faucet. They've got a bathtub and a toilet right in the house."

"Scottsbluff sure is growing," said Papa. "Cecil told me that the population is nearly three thousand now. I stopped at the Presbyterian church for a few minutes. It was good to see the minister again. He said he misses us, especially the children. All your cousins asked about you in the grocery store."

"I sure had a good time today," said Howard. "I met the family that moved into our old house. And when I saw Ralph, I asked if anyone had been put in jail lately. He said a few drunks, but there's been no big excitement since all those boys were thrown in a year ago for stealing watermelons."

"Papa, when we raise watermelons, will kids come to try to steal them?" I asked.

"We'll just have to wait and see," Papa said.

"I wonder when I'll get to town," Mamma said as she stacked the supper dishes. "When I go, I hope I'm not dumped in the road like you were."

School Days

NEBRASKA LAW REQUIRED that all children attend school until they were sixteen or until they had completed the eighth grade. Rural schools went only through the eighth grade, and to get into high school students from these schools had to pass state-prepared tests in fourteen subjects.

Students from the Lake Alice area who wanted to attend high school had to arrange for room and board in Scottsbluff during the school week. (Scottsbluff was about ten miles away, and this was too far to go every day by horse and buggy.) Because this cost money, and older children were needed at home to help with chores, few farm children went on to high school.

On Monday morning, Howard dressed quickly in his school clothes. His knickers, which had buckled below his knees last spring, now had to be fastened above the knees. He put on the new blue cotton shirt Mamma had made on her Singer sewing machine. She had made the buttonholes by hand and had put a tuck in the sleeves so she could let them down when they got too short. And he put on his new shoes.

Mamma made peanut butter and jelly sandwiches for Howard's lunch. She lined a five-pound syrup pail with part of a page from the Omaha *Daily News* and carefully laid the sandwiches in the bottom. Next she put in a small red apple and three homemade ginger cookies. On top she put a collapsible metal drinking cup and a square of newspaper to be used as a napkin.

"Be sure to eat the sandwiches first," Mamma said as she handed the lunch pail to Howard. "It's two and a half miles to the school. When you get to the top of the hill, maybe you'll see some other children. Look for the schoolhouse. The teacher should have the flag flying."

Howard stood on one foot and then the other, waiting for Mamma to stop talking.

"Here's your last year's report card. Don't lose it. That tells your teacher you've been passed to the second grade."

Howard left for school at eight o'clock with his lunch pail in one hand and his slate in the other. The slate was eight by ten inches, with a wooden frame that was painted red. In his shirt pocket he carried a piece of white chalk and a rag for erasing.

"Can I go tomorrow after he knows how to get to school?"

"No, you aren't old enough. You're only five. You have to be six."

"But I want to go," I insisted. "I want to eat my lunch in a bucket."

"Well, maybe I can do something about the lunch. Run to the cellar and find a pail like Howard's. I'll fix your lunch just like his. You may eat it at twelve o'clock. That's when he'll eat his."

Howard followed the fence for three-quarters of a mile.

Then the fence turned west. Howard remembered that Papa had said that the school was south from home, but he also remembered that he was to follow the fence, so he followed it. When he reached the top of the hill he could see many farmhouses, but no flag flying. He just kept walking. Finally he found a farmer in a field.

"Oh, the school is way over there," said the farmer, pointing to the southeast. "Go on down to the main road and then turn south. When you get to the first corner, go east for a mile. That's where you should have gone. At that corner, go another mile south, then go east again for about a quarter of a mile. . . . That's a long walk for a boy your size. How old are you?"

"I'm seven. I'll be eight in January. Thank you for helping me. I guess I'll be late for school."

By the time he reached school, it was nearly eleven o'clock. All the children stared at him when he entered the small white building. The teacher, Mrs. Jones, walked from the blackboard to the door to greet him. She showed him where to put his lunch and cap, and pointed to an empty seat.

"I'm in the second grade. Here's my report card."

She quickly scanned the card. "We don't have anyone in the second grade this year. . . . Let me hear you read."

Mrs. Jones and all the children in the room listened as Howard read aloud from a Brooks' Reader. "You're an excellent reader. I'll put you in the third grade. That will make four third graders."

All the children were dismissed for lunch at twelve. Those who lived nearby went home to eat, but some had come from as far as five miles away. The ones who stayed stopped at the pump to fill their drinking cups and went to a grassy spot under a big cottonwood tree. Five children had ridden horseback to school, and one girl had driven a pony hitched to a cart. All those who owned animals fed and watered them during the lunch period.

All grades were dismissed for the day at four o'clock. It was after five when Howard reached home.

Mamma didn't seem to be surprised that Howard had been put in the third grade. "You can manage it, I'm sure," she said. "Last year your first-grade teacher complained to me that she couldn't keep you busy."

After Howard had been in school for a month, Mrs. Jones was replaced by a new teacher, Mr. Johnson. Then, one afternoon in January, Howard came bursting into the tents at about two o'clock. When Mamma asked why he was home so early, he said breathlessly, "There isn't any more school today. The big boys threw Mr. Johnson out the window."

Mamma and Papa were upset, as were many of the other pupils' parents. Mr. Johnson refused to return to the school, but the parents felt he was not a good teacher anyway, so another new teacher was hired. Miss Miller had just completed her first semester at a teachers' college, which qualified her as a rural teacher under Nebraska state law. She had earned twelve hours of college credit and had passed state tests in seventeen subjects.

Although she stood only five feet two inches tall and some of the pupils were not much younger than herself, Miss Miller took charge right away and had all the pupils—even the big boys—hard at work from the very first day. Howard liked her very much, and Papa and Mamma said she must be a good teacher.

I looked forward to having a good teacher when I started school, but I was disappointed when I realized this meant I wouldn't get to see a teacher thrown out the window.

Merlan and Edna Adams, 1904.

Merlan and Edna Adams, 1915.

*Treva (standing), Howard, and Dorothy in
1914, before the move to the homestead.*

*Dorothy, December, 1915. On the left is the boiler
on the sled, for hauling snow to do the family wash.*

Dorothy, Treva, and Howard, December, 1915.

The Adams family—from left, Dorothy, Edna, Merlan, Howard, Treva—in front of their tent home, December, 1915. The smaller tent, where the cooking was done, is on the right, with stovepipes.

The Adams family on the bluff to the south of their homestead, December, 1915.

*Pleasant Valley School,
District No. 38, fall, 1914.
Treva had not yet started
school; Howard, wearing a
light-colored cap, is the third
boy from the left, behind the
first little girl.*

*Treva, Helen, Howard, and
Dorothy, 1917.*

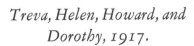

The homestead, 1917. The photograph was colored by hand and is torn and faded, but it shows the soddy (on the right) and other improvements—cattle (left),

windmill, and trees (right). Merlan and Helen are at
the left, in front of the windmill; on the right, Howard,
Treva, Edna, and Dorothy.

A base burner (left), a walking plow (above), and a farm wagon from an early Montgomery Ward catalogue.

Getting Ready for Winter

By the middle of September there was a chill in the air. Howard wore a jacket to school, and I put on my shoes every day. Mamma no longer rolled up the sides of the large tent in the morning. Instead, she started a wood fire in our base burner to keep the tent warm enough for Dorothy.

One evening in late September, Papa announced, "We can pick potatoes for our winter supply this Saturday at the Ritter farm. Bill said the men he hires never pick all the spuds, and we can take what they miss. He figures we can get at least twenty bushels. I can borrow a team and wagon from the irrigation district to get them home." He added, "I also learned today that there'll be just one more week of irrigation."

"That means you'll be out of a job," said Mamma.

"Yes, for a while anyway. It may be a good thing. There's lots to be done around here before winter sets in."

The farm was a busy place when we arrived on Saturday morning. Bill Ritter used a four-horse team to pull the potato digger. He had to start working at sunup to have enough rows dug by the time the pickers began their day at about seven o'clock.

The pickers were transients who bummed their way into Scottsbluff on the Burlington Railroad for the harvest. Their pay was twenty-five cents an hour and a bunkhouse to sleep in. They had the use of a stove and a few cooking utensils. Their diet consisted mostly of free spuds and black coffee. It took them about a week to complete the potato harvest at each farm.

The pickers filled half-bushel wire baskets with potatoes and dumped them into gunny sacks that stood about every thirty feet along the row. Each sack held a bushel and a half. Bill Ritter's sixteen-year-old son went through the field with a wagon, loading the full sacks. He hauled them to a large cellar where he dumped the spuds into bins for winter storage. For about an hour before quitting time, all the pickers helped him get the last sacks into the cellar.

I entertained Dorothy while Mamma, Papa, and Howard gleaned the fields. They went along the rows where the pickers had finished. They filled twenty sacks with potatoes, and it was nearly dark when we left for home.

The first morning Papa was off work, he said, "Those ten hens can't sit out on the prairie this winter. I'd better get busy and build them a home."

He took odds and ends of boards and pieces of tin and made the walls and roof of a small building. Then he covered it with dirt. Next he nailed together a couple of twelve-inch boards about three feet long to make a door. He showed me how to stand it against the opening of the hen house and brace it with a two-by-four. Then he stood back to admire the new house.

"We'll have to catch the hens and put them in for a couple of nights so they'll know the place belongs to them. Of course, we'll let them out every day that it's warm enough. I'll put the nests in there too."

"And you'd better do something about *our* door," Mamma reminded him. "The canvas cover over the screen just isn't enough." So Papa made a wooden door and covered it with canvas. And he made a latch so the door could be opened from either side.

Papa thought that cold air would come in under the tents and make the floor cold, so he borrowed a team and wagon to bring home a load of boards from the lumberyard in Scottsbluff. With the lumber he framed the tent all the way around. Then he shoveled earth against the boards.

One evening Papa saw a notice of a farm sale in the local newspaper. The farm owner was selling his animals, farm equipment, and household furnishings. "Guess I'll go to the sale," Papa told Mamma. "I might find something there we could say is your birthday present."

"How old will you be on your birthday?" Howard asked Mamma.

"You're not supposed to ask a lady how old she is, but since I'm your mother, I'll tell you. I'll be twenty-seven."

Tuesday morning Papa and Betsy left for the sale. "Don't buy something foolish, Merlan," Mamma warned him. "You know we don't have any money to waste."

"Now, Edna, don't worry. What I have in mind will be very useful. It's something that will make your work easier, and something all of us will enjoy. I'll see you about three o'clock."

Mamma sang one song after another all day. And it seemed to me that she went outdoors more than usual. She went after wood for the fires even though there was a pile by each stove.

Finally we saw him coming. "He's got something behind him across Betsy's back," said Mamma. "I can't imagine what it is."

"It's black and it's long. What is it, Mamma? Do you want something black?"

"It's a roll of something. I think just the outside is black."

Papa jumped from Betsy's back. He carefully lowered the roll. I didn't know what it was, but Mamma did. "It's linoleum! Oh, Merlan, you are so right. It will make my work easier. And best of all, it'll make the floor warmer."

Papa moved the dining table to the side of the tent and carefully unrolled the linoleum. It had blue and yellow squares. It covered nearly the whole floor.

"Now we won't have to shake sacks in the morning," said Mamma happily.

Nearly every Sunday friends came to visit. Many worried about our plan to live in the tents all winter. Often they brought gifts of food. As one guest lifted kettles from her buggy, she said, "We didn't have any way to let you know we were coming. I didn't want you to spend all our visiting time cooking, so I just brought enough for all of us."

The Saturday before Thanksgiving, Carl Bailey drove into the yard with a load of coal.

"Now, before you say anything, Merlan, let me do the talking," he said. "I know you have two big piles of wood, but when winter sets in, that won't be enough. You have more than your pride to think about. You've got three little kids. It'll be twenty below zero before the winter is over. You've got to have a good fire twenty-four hours every day, and driftwood won't hold the heat in your stoves all night."

Papa didn't say anything. He just looked at the woodpile.

"When I was at the lumberyard last week, the manager asked about you. He said you'd been in after a load of lumber. We got to talking, and he suggested you'd better have a load of coal. I told him I'd deliver it free if he'd sell it to you on time. So here it is."

Papa stood looking down at the wood. He pushed his old felt hat to the back of his head and said, "I really don't know what to say, Carl. You know it's always been my policy to pay my own way." He sighed. "I guess you're right, though. I do have to think about my family. Old Santa will be coming around before long, and I guess we'd better have it warm for him. So all I can say right now is a great big thank you."

Papa and Carl shoveled the coal into a pile near the south side of our home. "It'll be dark before I get back to town," Carl said. "The days are sure getting shorter. Have a good Thanksgiving."

"Thanks again," Papa said as he shook hands with his friend. "I'll return the favor when I can."

Papa carried a bucket of coal into the tent. "Edna, we'll make out all right," he said. "There are so many people trying to help us."

"The good Lord is helping too," said Mamma. "We have so much to be thankful for."

The day before Thanksgiving we had our first big snow-storm. It began at about ten o'clock with large flakes. By noon the wind had come up and the flakes were smaller. "Always remember, when the flakes are little the snow will continue," Papa said. "This should be a good day to get a goose for Thanksgiving. The ducks and geese will be flying low, trying to find protection from the storm."

He put on a heavy hunting jacket and his overshoes. He pulled down the fur-lined earflaps of his corduroy cap. The flaps fitted tightly over his ears, and the bill was nearly down to his eyebrows. He took his shotgun and went out into the snow.

Papa was gone for about two hours. When he returned, he looked like Santa Claus. Snow clung to his eyebrows and his cheeks were rosy. "Here's your turkey," Papa said, laughing, as he held up a twelve-pound goose.

It was a beautiful Thanksgiving morning. The prairie was covered with snow and the wind had stopped blowing. The temperature had dropped to nearly zero, but we were snug inside.

"It's such a special day. I'm going to do something I've wanted to do for a long time," Mamma told us. She lifted the lid of her old trunk and took out her lovely linen tablecloth and napkins.

"You're just making extra work for yourself. That goose and pumpkin pie will taste just as good on a table covered with oilcloth," said Papa.

"I want the children to learn good table manners," Mamma said as she unfolded the cloth and laid it on the table. "Now that the snow has come, we shouldn't have as much dust. Maybe we'll use the linens every Sunday from now on." She laid the napkins beside the plates. "With the colorful linoleum and the pretty table, I can almost forget we're having Thanksgiving dinner in a tent," she said.

Christmas

During December, I spent most of my waking hours looking at the Montgomery Ward catalogue. Howard and I called it our wish book, because we wished for so many of the things in it.

"Will Santa Claus bring me a doll with real hair, Mamma?"

"You'll just have to wait and see. Papa and I have to give the money to Santa Claus, and we don't have very much to give him this year."

"Won't I get anything?" I asked anxiously.

"Oh, yes, but not all the things you're finding in that catalogue."

Our mailbox was at the corner of a main road a mile and a quarter south of our home. Howard brought the newspaper and the letters each evening when he returned from school.

"Here's a letter from Grandma Adams," he said one evening in December.

Mamma read it aloud. It said: "I have sent a big wooden box

filled with a variety of surprises that should arrive soon after you get this letter. We hope you won't get too cold in that tent this winter. Love to all, Grandma."

A few days later we got a notice that the box had arrived at the freight office in Scottsbluff. It was time for Papa to go after supplies anyway, so he borrowed a wagon and a horse to team with Betsy. He left soon after breakfast for the long cold trip to town.

He came back that evening with groceries and the box Grandma Adams had sent. He pulled out the nails and took off the lid of the box. On top were the Christmas presents. Each was wrapped in colored paper, tied with ribbon, and labeled with a name tag. Mamma said, "We won't read the names on them now. That will make more surprises."

Under the presents were six long dresses. Papa's sisters sent Mamma the clothes they didn't want, for her to wear or to make over for Dorothy and me.

Papa found a pair of trousers in the box. He said as he held them up, "Mother must have sneaked these away from Dad. I hope they had a good harvest so he can buy some new ones. I've heard of people giving away the shirt off their backs, but this is giving the pants off their legs. Poor Dad."

In the bottom of the box were books for everyone. At the very bottom was a big book filled with maps of the world. Papa told us it was an atlas.

Papa had set a lot of traps, and during December he had caught many muskrats and coyotes. He could sell the muskrat skins for a dollar each, and a good coyote hide brought about twenty dollars.

The Sunday before Christmas a man drove his Model T Ford into the yard. He wanted two matching coyote skins to give his wife for Christmas, so she could have them made into a fur piece.

"If you've got skins I like, I'll give you twenty-five dollars apiece for them," the man told Papa.

About half an hour later Papa came in with five ten-dollar bills. "The man said he'd never seen such beautiful pelts," he told us. "I guess this cold weather is good for something. It makes heavy coats on the animals."

The last days before Christmas were busy ones. Mamma spent a lot of time at her sewing machine, turning the dresses from the box into clothes for us. Each day when I awoke from my nap, the tent was filled with good smells, but Mamma wouldn't tell me what she had been cooking.

One evening Papa came in carrying a goose. "I seem to be lucky just before the holidays," he said. "This one isn't quite as big as the Thanksgiving goose, but it feels like it's fatter. People must have left plenty of corn in their fields."

Before we went to bed on Christmas eve, Howard and I pulled our chairs out from the table. Each of us hung one of our long black stockings on a chair post.

Early the next morning we scrambled out of bed to find our stockings full. At the top of each was a popcorn ball with a narrow red ribbon around it. In the stockings were hard candy and peanuts. There was an orange in each toe and an apple in each heel. On my chair were new black stockings, a red dress, and a red stocking cap with a fluffy white tassel at the end. And Grandma had sent a beautiful doll with two dresses.

Howard got two new shirts, new black stockings, and a brown knitted cap. It had a turned-up cuff three inches wide. Howard put the cap on, and when he unrolled this cuff it came down to his shoulders. There was an oval opening for his eyes. "I guess my nose won't get cold now," he said.

Grandma had sent one surprise package especially for Howard and me. In it was a blackboard on legs. There was a chalk and eraser holder at the bottom. The best part was that there were lots of pictures on a roller at the top. There were people, animals, toys, trees, flowers, and buildings, and each had its name written underneath. All you had to do was turn the crank to find the picture you wanted to copy.

Mamma made the table look pretty with her linens. After we had eaten our goose, she brought a big plate of spice and sugar cookies to the table, and I knew what had made the house smell so good before Christmas.

We had just finished eating when the Harding family came to visit. Soon after they arrived, Mr. Harding said, "Mrs. Adams, when we helped you move here last August, you said you would tell me about your old clocks sometime."

"All right, but let me pop a dishpan full of corn first."

Each of us was given a small bowl heaped with buttered corn, and Mamma started her story. Howard and I had heard it many times, but we always looked forward to hearing it again.

"I was the youngest of six children," said Mamma. "My mother and one brother died of typhoid fever when I was just four years old. My older brother and two sisters had left home. Papa didn't think he could manage a job and keep house for my eight-year-old brother and me. So Roy went to live with some cousins in Omaha, and I was sent to live with my mother's parents in Iowa.

"Grandpa Moats was a wagon maker and a preacher. Every Sunday I had to sit in the front row at church to listen to Grandpa preach. I didn't understand what he was saying, but at home he always said, 'Little girls are to be seen and not heard,' so I sat as quiet as I could.

"There weren't any little children in the neighborhood, so I always had to play by myself. The only thing I remember doing that I enjoyed was visiting the big old clocks on the second floor. There were three grandfather clocks in the upper hall. And in one spare bedroom there were four more. These are two of them," she said, looking up at the clocks on top of the china cupboard.

"Those clocks were my friends. No one ever wound them except me. I climbed on a chair to start them. I didn't know how to make the time right, so they struck different hours at the same time, or at intervals of a few minutes. I didn't mind. I thought it was like music. I would talk to the clocks, and they seemed to answer me.

"When I was twelve my father decided he could keep me again. My grandparents asked if I wanted to take anything with me. I chose these," she said, looking again at her treasures. "My father said the wooden cases were hand carved. The word *Schwarz* is cut into the wood. That means they came from the Black Forest in Germany."

"Now I know why you told me to handle them with care," Mr. Harding said as he rose from his chair. "It's been a wonderful visit, but it's time to get home. Cows have to be milked and eggs have to be gathered on Christmas, just like every other day."

Mamma said, "Thank you for coming. It has helped to make our first Christmas on the homestead a wonderful one."

Winter Passes

THAT FIRST WINTER WAS COLD, with many snowstorms. Often Mamma wouldn't let Howard walk the two and a half miles to school. "We don't know what this storm will turn into," she would say. "You could get lost in a blizzard."

After Papa had stopped riding ditch at the end of September, he had brought water from the lake in a wooden barrel on the sled for washing clothes and cleaning. When winter came, and the snow piled high in drifts, Howard and I filled the boiler with snow. We would put the boiler on the little sled that Papa had made for us and pull it from drift to drift. When we came home, Mamma put the boiler on the stove until the snow melted. Then she poured it into the washtub. We had to fill the boiler several times before there was enough water for the family wash. We used melted snow for our Saturday night baths, too.

Papa shot ducks, geese, and rabbits for the table. One time he killed thirteen ducks with only two shots. Before the winter was over we had eaten 135 ducks. Mamma saved the feathers from the undersides of the birds and made pillows and feather beds for all of us.

Cottontails and jackrabbits were plentiful. About a week before Papa went to town for supplies, he shot all the rabbits he could find. After skinning them, he hung the carcasses on the clothesline to freeze. There was a grocery store in a Negro section of Scottsbluff that paid fifteen cents for each one.

Papa went to farm sales during January and February. He bought a walking plow, a wagon, a harness, and two horses. Jim had been a racehorse in his younger days and was broken for riding or driving. Dick was young and only halter broke. Betsy had been loaned to Papa for two years, and that time had come to an end. It was a sad day for all of us when Papa returned her to her owner, Mr. Raymond. But life was a little easier now that we had our own team and wagon. Papa could go to town for supplies without having to borrow an extra horse and wagon. And the team pulled our big sled, loaded with two large wooden barrels of lake water, right to the tent door. We could use water more freely now, and Mamma was pleased that she wouldn't have to go to the lake to do the wash next summer.

"I remember my grandfather used to say, 'You never miss the water till the well runs dry.' I never realized how much water I used until we didn't have a well. How long will it be, Merlan, before you have one drilled?"

"I understand the quarter section on the west of us will be open sometime the first of next year," said Papa. "I'll file for it, and if there's a chance we'll get it, we'll have the well drilled. We really need 320 acres to make a good living here.

We can expect some dry years when we won't have a bountiful harvest."

In February, we had been living on the homestead for six months. "The time for settlement has expired," Papa told us. "I guess we'll never know who drove the third stake at the corners."

"Papa, is the land ours now?" Howard asked.

"It will be if we stay here three years and fulfill all the requirements. We have to build a house, plant a garden, and fence the land. And we'll need to dig a well, plant potatoes and grain, and build a barn and chicken house."

During that first winter on the homestead, we became acquainted with Ralph and Lucy Harris. Their 160 acres adjoined ours on the east. Ralph came from Kansas. He had built a two-room sod house before he brought Lucy to the homestead.

"I helped my father build a soddy when I was twelve," he told Papa. "Whenever you get ready to build yours, I'll help you."

"Thanks. Is this good sod for a house?"

"The best. It's far better than in Kansas. Here the roots of the prairie grass intertwine so thickly, it's hard to cut the sod apart. You need have no fear that heavy rains will hurt the walls of your home."

"What kind of plow will I need to cut the sod?"

"Your walking plow is fine. Just be sure the plowshare is very sharp."

Papa went back to work for the irrigation district the first of March. He helped to clean and repair the irrigation canals and ditches before they were filled with water in May.

In his off hours, Papa plowed an area for a huge garden. Mamma hoed and raked the plowed ground until the soil was fine. When she peeled potatoes for cooking she made the skins very thick. She cut the skins into pieces, with at least one eye in each piece. Then she planted the pieces in the garden about four inches deep and a foot apart. She planted peelings from April until the first of July. This was the beginning of a business for which Papa was to be known as "Spud" Adams in many middle western states in future years.

School was out in early May, because spring was a busy time for everyone on the farm. Children were needed at home to thin beets, hoe weeds, and cut potatoes for planting. Mamma was glad to have Howard's help in the garden.

One day a well-dressed man came to our home. He tethered his gray horse to the barbed-wire fence, climbed through the wires, and strode rapidly toward our tent.

"That's Mr. Watson," said Mamma. "You children stand here beside me."

We had heard Papa and Mamma talking about Mr. Watson. He was a wealthy farmer-rancher who had pastured his cattle on our homestead in previous years. He wanted to go on using the land for pasture, so he didn't want us to live here.

"Don't you children say anything," Mamma cautioned as he approached.

"Good morning, Mrs. Adams. May I talk to your husband?" said Mr. Watson.

Mamma shoved her hands deep into her apron pockets and stood up very straight. "He's not here. What do you want? I'm sure I can answer your questions," she said firmly.

"You were lucky your tent wasn't blown away when the Pattersons lost their house in the tornado," he said. "You know you're a long way from a doctor, and your children can get bitten by rattlesnakes."

Mamma said pointedly, "Mr. Watson, just what is the purpose of your visit?"

"I'm prepared to give you one hundred dollars if you will move off this land right away."

"Mr. Watson, we lived through our first winter in fine shape. Not one of us even had a cold. I see no reason for us to move. We are staying. Anyway—that is our plan now. Until we see our children suffering, we are staying. Good day, Mr. Watson."

The caller tipped his Stetson hat, turned on his heel, and returned to his waiting horse.

Summer

I TURNED SIX YEARS OLD on June 27, 1915. I didn't have a party, since there were no children my age living nearby. Instead, I went to town with Papa. It had been more than a year since I'd been to Scottsbluff.

On the way we passed the old construction camp where the screened-in meat shed had been my playhouse. When we got to town, Papa went to do the shopping and left me to spend the day with our old friends the Edwards family. They had two daughters near my age who had been my friends when we'd lived in town.

That day was the first time I ever saw water piped into a house. I thought the Edwardses must be very rich to afford hot and cold water. I wanted to take a bath in their bathtub, but I was afraid to ask them.

We had a good dinner, and to my surprise Mrs. Edwards had a cake for me with six pink candles. It was a wonderful day. The best part of the whole trip was showing Lotus and

Olive Edwards that I had learned how to whistle, when they couldn't do it.

A few days later, Mamma told me that the Harrises had a baby girl who'd been born on my birthday. And one afternoon in July, Mamma put Dorothy in her buggy and the three of us walked the mile to visit little Laura and her mother. It was the first time I'd been to the Harris home. I couldn't keep my eyes off the beautiful sheer curtains over the bedroom windows.

On the way home, I asked, "Can we have pink curtains at our windows?"

"We'll just have to wait and see," said Mamma. "I thought they were very pretty, too."

"Mamma, they have a wooden floor."

"We'll have one too when we build our house," said Mamma.

"When will we have a house?"

"Before Christmas, I hope."

All summer the rains came just as they were needed. We had such a bountiful garden we were able to give some vegetables to the Harrises.

Mamma dried sweet corn and stored it in a flour sack. We raised enough potatoes for our winter supply. We had plenty of carrots and turnips, which we stored in a pile of sand in the cellar to keep them fresh. Mamma tied the brown stems of the onions together and hung them up to dry.

Mamma canned green beans in glass jars. She set the jars on a rack in the wash boiler, covered them with water, and boiled them for three hours.

One whole row in the garden was just flowers. We had poppies, cosmos, and bachelor's buttons.

In early May, yellow and purple sweet peas and bluebells

began to bloom on the prairie. Before the month was over, purple Johnny-jump-ups appeared in protected areas in the hills. Bluebonnets covered the prairie in June. From June through August the morning glory bushes were covered with red blossoms each morning. In July I strung the bulbs of yellow soapweed blossoms on a string to make necklaces. When I wore them I had to hold my nose, because they smelled terrible.

On hot days, large schools of carp and suckers would come near the shore of the lake. I tried to catch them with my hands, but they always wiggled free. Papa showed Howard and me how to catch them with a pitchfork. When we speared the four-tine fork among them, one or two were pinned to the bottom of the lake. We tipped the fork carefully to release one fish at a time. We put them in a gunny sack to carry them home.

We piled wood for the stoves. Papa said, "I know we'll need to buy coal again, but the wood doesn't cost any money."

Papa built a wooden barn for Jim and Dick. It was big enough for at least four horses and a few cattle. "We've got to look to the future," he said.

School
at Last

FINALLY THE DAY ARRIVED when school was to start.

I had new black buttoned shoes and long white stockings
that Mamma had ordered from the Montgomery Ward
catalogue. Mamma had made over several of the dresses from
the Christmas box for me, and I put one of them on. She made
curls all around my head by brushing my wet hair around her
finger. She made the hair on the top of my head into two curls
that she tied with a ribbon to match my dress.

My lunch pail was filled with an apple, cookies, jelly
sandwiches, and a little jar of soup beans. I had a folding
drinking cup like Howard's. Since he was in the fourth grade,
he carried a new tablet and the slate was mine.

The year before, Howard had worn a path on the prairie
between our house and the main road, one and a quarter miles
south. He and I had used the trail all summer when we went
after the mail.

As soon as we reached the main road we were joined by

other children. I met a girl named Maureen and her brother. Maureen had long braids that reached nearly to her waist. She was in the second grade.

When we entered the schoolhouse Maureen showed me where to put my lunch pail. Then I met Miss Miller. She was pretty, with dark hair pulled straight back in a neat roll. She wore a red and white gingham dress and high-button black shoes.

"This is my sister, Amy," said Miss Miller. "She's also in the first grade. Maybe you girls would like to share a desk."

Amy and I selected the second desk in the row for first graders.

Except for the eight first graders, everyone seemed to know what to do after we saluted the flag. Miss Miller helped us with arithmetic and put some problems on the blackboard for us to copy and add.

When I looked up from my work, I saw the boy across the aisle open his inkwell and push the end of one of Maureen's braids into the ink. I yelled out loud for the teacher. Maureen turned her head quickly. Her braids swung through the air, throwing ink on herself and her seatmate.

Miss Miller scolded the boy and shook him. Then she told the girls to go out to the pump and try to wash off the ink. It came off their faces, but not their clothes.

When recess time came, Miss Miller asked me to stay in·my seat. She told me very quietly that next time I saw something going on I should try to let her know without frightening the others.

When we arrived home that afternoon, Howard informed Mamma, "Treva wasn't in school an hour before she let everyone know she was there. Some of the boys told me they were sure glad she wasn't their sister." Mamma told me the same things Miss Miller had, and I promised I'd try to remember not to yell aloud in school again.

The water was shut out of the irrigation ditches at the end of September. On our way to and from school, some of us thought it was fun to run through an empty ditch instead of crossing the bridge. The sides were steep so it was easy to slide down into the ditch, but we had to be pulled out on the other side by friends standing on the bank. One day Howard and the other boys told Maureen and me that there was a bird's nest under the bridge. When we came back from looking for it, we saw Maureen's lunch pail start to move. We were scared until Howard took the lid off, and out jumped a frog. Maureen was furious. The other boys were always playing tricks on her, but for some reason she hadn't expected it of Howard.

Before the weather turned cold, Mamma sent another order to Montgomery Ward. I got high-buckled overshoes and warm red mittens to match my stocking cap. Mamma's sister in Pennsylvania sent a box of outgrown clothes of my cousin's. She was two years older than I. Her coat and pretty dresses fitted me perfectly.

As the days grew shorter we left for school before the sun came up, and it was nearly dark before we returned in the afternoon. In cold weather my curls, still wet from Mamma's comb, froze stiff and then turned white with frost. When we met other children they'd greet me with, "Hello, Granny. Aren't you too old to go to school?" or, "Howard, who's that old lady with you today?"

The ravines we had to cross in the first mile of our walk were often filled with snow. When it was frozen hard, it was fun to slide across the top of the ravines and drifts. But when it had just fallen, I would sink in up to my knees and my lunch pail would drag across the snow. Howard would have to come back and pull me out.

Before Christmas I heard that in January we would be attending a new school three miles east of the old one. I was worried about having to walk three more miles, but Maureen reassured me. A school bus would pick us up by our mailbox, she said.

On January 16, 1916, the new Lake Alice school was opened. The night before, we all took our books home from the little country school so we could take them to the new school. The new school was large and exciting. The first and second grades had a whole room to themselves, and Miss Miller was there.

the Soddy

It was nearly the last of October, 1915, when Papa said to Mamma, "I've arranged with Ralph to meet me on the thirty-first at the foot of our big bluff."

"That's Mamma's birthday," I said. "What are you going to do up by the big hill?"

"I'll start cutting the sod for our house," Papa told me. "I know that's what your mother wants most for her birthday."

On that Sunday morning Papa loaded the walking plow into the wagon and tied the big sled behind. Dorothy and Mamma rode with Papa, and Howard and I ran ahead.

Ralph Harris was waiting for us. He helped Papa unhitch Jim and Dick from the wagon; then they unloaded the plow and hitched the team to it.

"Keep your furrows straight," Ralph cautioned. "That will save a lot of work in making your walls nice and straight. Try to make all the sod four inches thick."

As Papa tied the ends of the reins together, he said, "Edna

has often said, 'All that you do, do with your might; things done by half are never done right.' " Then he put the reins over his head, across his shoulders, and under his right arm. He grasped the handles of the plow and said, "Get up." The horses walked steadily forward and the first layer of sod was turned over. Just as Ralph had said, the black roots of the grass were thickly intertwined.

When the strip he was cutting was about a hundred yards long, Papa stopped the horses. He brought a straight-edged spade from the wagon and cut the sod into slabs eighteen inches long and a foot wide. Howard helped Ralph pull the sled over to the furrow and load the slabs onto the sled. The horses were hitched to the sled and hauled it over to the tents, where the sod was stacked on the ground. Before noon they had enough cut and hauled to begin the walls of our house.

The men stopped work for lunch, but Papa was so anxious to get the job done that he left the table before dessert. Ralph said, "I know you're anxious to get into your house, but don't try to build it in one day, Merlan. Another good saying is 'Haste makes waste.' "

"Of course you're right, Ralph, but I'll sleep better tonight if I know how the house is going to look."

Papa and Ralph carefully formed the four corners. The outside of the house measured twenty-four by thirty-eight feet. The walls would be three feet thick, so, inside, the house would measure eighteen by thirty-two feet. The thick walls would make the house strong as well as cool in summer and warm in winter.

"As soon as I can afford it, I'll add a kitchen on the north, so I'll put the door here," Papa said as he stepped off the space for the doorway. "As the family grows, we'll need another room, so I'd better make a window on this side, too. It will be easy to change it into a door for the entrance into the new room."

"I want a big double window in the south," Mamma said. "That'll let in the sun, and I'll fill the windowseat with potted flowers."

"We want the morning sunshine, too, so we'll have an east window," Papa said.

Mamma planned to use the northeast corner of the house for the kitchen and dining area. The beds would go along the west wall. Papa decided he would put just a half window in the west. "Most of our storms will come from that direction," he said, "and I don't want any drafts over our beds."

Papa laid boards to mark the spaces for the windows and door. And from then on, he worked nearly every day cutting, hauling, and piling the sod. He used a plumb line to make sure the sides of our house were straight up and down. Each afternoon when Howard and I returned from school, we filled our little wagon with pieces of sod Papa had trimmed from the walls of the house with a big butcher knife, and hauled them away.

Slow but sure, the walls reached a height of eight feet. At the ends of the house, Papa built gables with peaks about two feet high. He used a four-by-six beam for the ridgepole, and two-by-eights for rafters. A ceiling could be nailed to them someday.

One evening Papa announced, "If it's good weather Sunday, some of our friends are coming to help put on the roof. I'll get some twelve-inch boards, tar paper, and a stack of sod. They think we can roof it in one day."

To our surprise, whole families came that Sunday. The women brought pies and kettles of food, and it was just like a big party. It was an unseasonably warm December day, and everyone stayed outdoors. We children played blindman's buff, drop the handkerchief, farmer in the dell, and pom-pom pullaway. The boys had a three-legged race.

By the time the sun went down the roof was on. "I really didn't think we could do it in one day," Papa said as he relaxed in his rocker that night. "Now it looks like we'll get into the soddy before Christmas. But we still have to lay the floor, put in the windows, and hang the door."

Two days before Christmas we moved into the soddy. Mamma was delighted with all the room after living for nearly a year and a half in the crowded tents.

"The lineoleum won't cover the whole floor," she said. "But I won't mind. At least there's a wooden floor I can sweep and scrub." After the dirt floors of the tents, having a floor she could really clean seemed like a luxury to Mamma.

In the kitchen area, Papa installed a used coal range he had bought for five dollars. It had a large oven, a five-gallon reservoir to heat water in, and a warming oven.

Papa had also bought a double bed for Dorothy and me at a farm sale. It and Mamma's and Papa's bed were placed end to end along the west wall. For the time being, Howard would sleep on the couch, which was placed near the big south window.

When we were all moved in, Dorothy and I settled down to play with our toys behind the big base burner in the southeast corner. Papa and Mamma rocked and talked in front of the warm fire. Howard sat on the couch whittling a little animal from a piece of soft wood.

"We have enough room to put up a trapeze for Howard and a swing for Dorothy," Papa said. "I bought the ropes a month ago. When I was a lad I could do more stunts than any boy in our neighborhood." He looked at Howard and continued,

"Every day I want you to practice chinning yourself. I'll teach you stunts, too."

"Where in the world do you expect to put them?" Mamma asked in astonishment.

"That middle rafter is just the place. I'll arrange it so that the ropes can to tied up above our heads when they aren't in use."

"If you can find room for a swing and trapeze, you can find room to make a hanger for our clothes," Mamma insisted.

It didn't take Papa long to figure out a way to fasten a ten-foot iron pipe along the north wall behind the head of their bed. This easily held all the clothes we had.

The next day, Papa and Mamma used the tents to line the walls. They cut the canvas into strips and fastened them to the walls with long nails. The light-colored tent canvas was much nicer to look at than the dirt walls had been, and it helped keep the room cleaner, too.

It was the day before Christmas, and Howard said to me, "If Santa can't find us this year, we're going to have a good Christmas anyway. We've got a new house."

On Christmas morning Howard found a note pinned to his stocking. It read: "You'll have to go outside to get one of your presents. It wouldn't go down the stovepipe."

We rushed outside. We didn't see anything until we looked upward. There was a .22 rifle fastened to the stovepipe. Howard was delighted with his gun. Papa put a tin can on top of the clothesline pole. He told Howard, "When you shoot a hole in that can from twenty-five feet away, you're ready to shoot a rabbit."

Dorothy and I both got china dolls. They had beautiful

dresses but funny-looking faces. Papa explained that Germany was at war, so Santa's helpers couldn't send us dolls from over there. Our dolls had been made in the United States by inexperienced helpers, he said.

Papa got a new pipe, and Mamma had new high-top shoes.

That evening Howard said, "I'm going to hang my stocking again tonight."

"Why?" I asked in surprise. "Santa only comes once, and that was last night. You won't get anything."

"Well, we'll see," he said.

As soon as we woke the next morning, we could see that Howard's stocking was full. As we scrambled out of bed, I cried, "You have to give me half!"

Howard found a note pinned on his stocking. It read: "I had a pony for you, but it got away."

The stocking was full of horse manure.

One day when Papa was away, Mamma went outside and pounded some hunks of sod with a hammer until they crumbled. She pulled out the roots and grass. Then she put the dirt in her colander and shook it through the holes.

"What are you doing?" I asked.

"It's a secret. You can watch me, but don't tell your father. I want to see if it works before he knows about it."

She added a little water at a time to the fine soil. Then she carried the mixture into the house. She lifted a strip of canvas behind the door. Using the pancake turner as a trowel, she plastered an area about two feet square. Then she dropped the canvas back into place.

A few days later, Mamma showed Papa the hard dry dirt plaster.

"Wonderful!" he said. "Now we'll finish all the walls."

They worked together until the whole room was plastered. And the next time Papa went to town, he bought a sack of dry cement. He mixed it with water and spread it over the mud plaster.

A few days later, Mamma looked through the samples of wallpaper in the catalogue. She chose one that had a white background with stripes of little blue and pink flowers running up and down. When it came, she made a paste by boiling together flour, sugar, and water, and then she papered the walls. When it was finished, we all thought our house was beautiful.

Later Papa divided the original soddy into two rooms and added two more, one built of sod and the other built of lumber.

Since very few people lived in sod houses at that time, many of our friends brought their guests to see ours. One day our lawyer, Mr. Scott, came with a Mrs. Post from Philadelphia.

"What a quaint house," she said. "It must be a happy place, because you have flowers blooming on the roof."

Mamma told her, "We've had a great deal of rain this spring. The wild flowers that grow on the prairie just kept on growing in the sod we used on our roof."

Mr. Scott explained to Mrs. Post how we'd built our house. He seemed as proud of our accomplishments as though he'd been working alongside us. Mamma invited them inside.

Mrs. Post quickly scanned the room, then turned to Mr. Scott. "It isn't as dirty on the inside, is it?" she observed.

Our home wasn't dirty—it was clean and neat. Mrs. Post's remark made me angry, and after she left I told Mamma, "I don't like her."

Joy and Sorrow

MAMMA BAKED BREAD twice each week. She started the mixture before breakfast with a cup of mashed potatoes, two cups of potato water, salt, sugar, lard, and a cake of yeast. After the breakfast dishes were done, she cleaned the dishpan well. Then she sifted flour into it. She didn't measure the flour, but she always seemed to know when she had enough. With her hand she'd scoop out a nest in the middle of the flour and put in the yeast mixture. Gently she worked the mixture and flour together. Then she placed the ball of dough in the middle of a floured area on the dining table and kneaded it.

Mamma always baked three loaves of bread, which fitted into one big pan. There was dough left over to be made into a pan of rolls for supper, a batch of donuts, or sweet cinnamon rolls. Sometimes she used the extra dough for a fourth loaf of bread.

In January, 1916, Papa received notice that the 160 acres to the west of us would be open for settlement in February.

He filed a claim for it. The same rules were to apply as in 1914, except there would be no race. "Another man came into the office to file while I was there," said Papa, "so it looks like there will be a contest again. . . . We'll have to put something there to show we claim it."

"Do we have to move our house over there?" I asked.

"Oh, no," Papa said, smiling. "I'll put the chicken house on a sled and the horses will pull it over. And Mr. Scott and two witnesses will be there."

On February 24, Howard and I stayed home from school. Papa and Howard hitched Jim and Dick to the sled and pulled the chicken house onto the new claim. Mamma, Dorothy, and I walked there with the lawyer and witnesses.

Near the lake, we saw a man with a sheepherder's wagon. He was the other claimant, busy getting himself located. Later we learned that his wife had refused to leave their home in town. Sometimes their fifteen-year-old son spent a few days with his father.

For the next few months, whenever Mamma baked, she would make a fourth loaf of bread. Then she'd tell Howard and me to take it and a pot of soup beans to the man in the sheepherder's wagon. I just couldn't understand why she did this. I knew the man was trying to get the same land that we were.

One time when we were carrying the food, I said to Howard, "Why does Mamma feed that man? If she didn't, maybe he'd leave. Then the land would be ours."

"Mamma feels sorry for him," said Howard.

One evening a farmer came to see Papa. He said he wanted to build a stone barn, and asked if he could take stones from that 160 acres.

"Of course," said Papa. "Go right ahead. You didn't have to ask me."

"Your neighbor chased me off the hill today when I came after a load of stones," said the farmer. "He said the land was his, and that if I wanted stones I'd have to pay for them."

Papa looked surprised. "That land still belongs to the United States government. It isn't any more his than mine. Help yourself to all the stones you want. He can't stop you."

One morning in late spring when we were eating breakfast, Papa announced, "Our neighbor is gone. When I took the horses down for a drink, his wagon wasn't there. He took everything."

Mamma said, "I'm relieved, but I really felt sorry for him."

"I wasn't surprised to find him gone," said Papa. "He hadn't done any plowing for a garden, or anything to show he wanted to establish a home."

Papa and Mamma became acquainted with Mr. and Mrs. Ticeny, a young couple who had come over from Europe. They had a new Overland touring car. One day Mrs. Ticeny invited Mamma to ride into Scottsbluff. Mamma was delighted to have a chance to go to town—she hadn't been there for almost two years. She enjoyed the ride, but was surprised when Mrs. Ticeny drove straight through Scottsbluff. Soon they were crossing the bridge over the North Platte River and heading for the next town, three miles away. Mamma thought this was strange, as Mrs. Ticeny hadn't said anything about going to Gering.

When they stopped in front of the courthouse, Mamma said, "I didn't know you'd planned to come to Gering. Do you have to go into the courthouse?"

Mrs. Ticeny looked at Mamma sheepishly and confessed that she had forgotten how to make the car stop, and had only just remembered.

They drove back to Scottsbluff, did their shopping, and returned home. That evening Mamma said, "I didn't get to see any of my friends, but I'll never forget this trip."

One morning Papa ran into the house calling, "Give me some hot water and Epsom salts! Jim has been bitten by a rattlesnake!"

We all followed Papa as he hurried back out the door. Our faithful Jim was lying on his side, pawing the air with his legs.

"Poor thing, he's in such pain," Mamma said as we looked at Jim's swollen head. His nose was twice its normal size, and his eyes were swollen shut.

Papa said, "Only a rattlesnake bite could have done this. I'll keep the plaster of hot salts on his head. It might help. Epsom salts are supposed to draw the poison out."

Jim's tongue was so big he couldn't close his mouth. Papa put drops of water on it in the hope that Jim might be able to swallow some.

Day and night Papa nursed the horse. Jim kept his legs in motion until he became so weak and exhausted that he seemed to fall asleep. I was sure Jim was going to die, and I was very unhappy. I visited him often and said over and over to him, "Get well, Jim. I love you. Please get well."

Finally, Papa came in one morning to tell us that Jim was up on his feet. It had taken nearly a week for the poison to leave his body. Gradually his head returned to normal size, but it was almost a month before he was strong enough to work again.

*　　*　　*

One day in May, Papa left the house as usual in the morning, but came home again before we left for school. Mrs. Wright was with him. "Your mother doesn't feel very well, so I'm going to stay home today," Papa said.

"Why is Mrs. Wright here?" I asked.

"Your mother might need her. Now you two scoot off to school. I expect there'll be a surprise when you get home."

I don't know when a day was so long. Howard and I ran most of the way home from the school bus stop. We burst into the house asking, "What's the surprise?"

"Listen," said Papa.

We listened. We heard a baby crying. Lying beside Mamma was our new sister, Helen Lucille.

Early one morning when Helen was less than two weeks old, Ralph Harris came across the prairie as fast as his horse could carry him.

He stopped long enough to ask in a voice filled with anguish, "Mrs. Adams, please hurry to our home. Laura is very ill. I'm going to the camp to call the doctor. Oh, do hurry!"

"Of course," Mamma assured him. "I'll go right away." She turned to Howard and me. "You'll have to stay with Dorothy and Helen until I get back." Mamma was just regaining her strength, but she rolled her long apron around her arms and began to run across the prairie.

She stayed at the Harrises' house until Ralph returned from making the telephone call. Then she came home to nurse Helen. We had already missed the bus, so we stayed home from school that day. Mamma went back to the Harrises', and when she returned the second time, she said sadly, "Little Laura died. The doctor came, but he couldn't save her."

I cried. Laura had been born on my birthday and had been very special to me.

Fulfilling Requirements

ONE DAY PAPA RETURNED from a farm sale with a milk cow. "We'll stake her out in a different place every day for grazing, and I'll take her to the lake each evening for a drink," he said.

A few days later Papa became very ill, with a high fever. He was bedfast for nearly a week. Instead of taking Bossy to the lake, we children brought water for her. "If she decided to run away, we couldn't hold her," Mamma said.

After Papa felt better, he decided he'd take Bossy to the lake. She started to run. Papa had been weakened by his illness and wasn't strong enough to hold her. Howard and I tried to help him, but Bossy kept on running. Finally Papa sat down, still holding the rope. Bossy pulled him several feet across the prairie before she stopped. Papa had been dragged over several beaver tail cacti.

Mamma pulled the cactus needles from Papa's hips and legs one by one. "I sure don't want another experience like that,"

Papa said. "I guess it's time to have a well dug and get some fences built."

In July, 1916, Jess came with his big drilling rig. He advised Papa to put the well close enough to the house so we could get water in a blizzard, but far enough away so that the water tank for the animals wouldn't be in the front yard. Papa decided to have the well about thirty feet northeast of the house.

When Jess had drilled sixty feet he hit water. "I'd better go another fifteen feet," he said. "Then you'll always have water, even in dry years."

Soon the pump was completed. It had a three-foot cement platform all the way around it. Before the summer was over, Papa bought a used windmill and a galvanized metal water tank seven feet in diameter and three feet deep. He built a corral for the animals and put the tank in one corner. A two-inch pipe carried the water from the pump to the tank.

Mamma was delighted. Next to building the house, she thought drilling the well was the best thing we had done. After two years, she now had all the water she needed.

Although Papa worked for the irrigation district that summer, he also plowed enough land to raise half an acre of potatoes and half an acre of corn. When the garden needed water, Mamma let the windmill pump enough so that the stock tank overflowed. Howard and I made little ditches to carry the water to the plants.

Papa decided it was time to plant the shade trees he had always wanted. "I'd better plant some cottonwoods," he told us. "I've heard they're the fastest-growing tree in western Nebraska."

A friend of Papa's had planted a row of trees on his farm for a windbreak. He soon learned he'd planted them too close together. He told Papa to take every other tree, to give the remaining trees more room. Papa came home with eight small cottonwoods and planted them on all four sides of the house.

When Howard went rabbit hunting, Mamma told me always to walk behind him. I did until we reached the big hill. Then I walked beside him so I could watch him shoot. One day I asked if I could try. He showed me how to hold the rifle and look through the sight before I pulled the trigger.

One day, to my surprise, I shot a rabbit. I carried it into the house and proudly told Mamma that I had killed it. She was unhappy that I hadn't always walked behind Howard, as she'd told me to, but she was proud that I'd learned to shoot.

Papa bought fourteen head of cattle and two more horses and completed the fencing of the 320 acres in 1917. That year he raised ten acres of corn, five acres of potatoes, half an acre of dry beans, and five acres of winter food for the animals.

Finally the three years required for homesteading had passed. Now Papa could begin to take the last steps to make the land legally ours.

the Certificate of Ownership

ON JULY 23, 1917, Papa went before Lewis L. Raymond, United States Commissioner at Scottsbluff within the Alliance land district, to file "a notice of intention to make final three-year proof to establish claim to the homestead" we had settled on August 17, 1914.

Mr. Raymond said a notice of Papa's intention had to be published in the Scottsbluff *Republican* for five consecutive weeks. For this Papa paid the newspaper seven dollars and fifty cents.

Early in September, Papa received notice that he was to appear in Mr. Raymond's office on September 18 and bring two witnesses.

Papa answered twenty questions. The testimony that was known as the "final proof" was then sent to the United States land office in Alliance.

Ralph Harris and my friend Maureen's father were asked eighteen questions. Each answered them separately, but in about the same way. They said that they had been on our homestead at least once each week during the three years since August, 1914, and that we'd always been there when they'd visited. They told how each year Papa had plowed more land and put up more buildings. Each said the total value of our improvements was between seven and eight hundred dollars.

The whole family was excited when Papa received the notice that we were to appear in Alliance on October 17.

Mr. Harding said, "Merlan, I moved you and your family onto this land, and now I'm going to take you to the federal courthouse in my Model T to complete this deal."

Papa said, "You know it's about sixty-five miles to Alliance. That means it'll be a three-day trip—a day to go over, a day to appear in court, and a day to come home."

"That's all right. Nothing is pushing on the farm right now."

Our lawyer, Mr. Scott, said he'd take Ralph Harris and Maureen's father, our two witnesses, in his car.

For the first forty miles we traveled over a rough trail that went through ranchland. Once we ran over a rattlesnake, and Howard got so excited that he jumped up and bumped his head on the cloth top of the car. "Did you see that rattlesnake?" he yelled. "We just ran over it!"

I'd never ridden very far in a car, and, with all the jolting, I became carsick. Howard gave me his place in the front seat, and soon I felt better.

In Alliance, we found a hotel near the courthouse. I was delighted to see a bathroom with a tub at the end of the hall. Mamma promised Howard and me that we could take baths that evening. Papa said we'd splurge and eat our meals in the hotel, just like rich people.

91

The next morning when we entered the courtroom, no one was there except our lawyer and the witnesses. At the front of the room was a desk on a high platform. There were several rows of long benches with high backs. On one wall was a picture of President Wilson, and there was a flag on a pole near the platform.

Very soon a man in a black robe came in. Mr. Scott stood, so we did, too, until the judge was seated at his desk.

My feet didn't touch the floor, so I had a hard time keeping from sliding off the slippery wooden bench.

"Mr. Adams," the judge said to Papa, "I have a record of the questions you answered in Mr. Raymond's office. Do you swear that you answered them truthfully?"

That sounded to me as if the judge thought Papa was a liar, and it made me mad. But Papa just said, "I do."

Then the judge asked him about the homestead. "What did you live in before you built your sod house in the fall of 1915?"

"The day of the settlement we set up two tents. We lived in them for sixteen months."

"I see that your house has two rooms."

"That's correct. As soon as I can afford it, I'll build a kitchen on the north. Someday I'll add a fourth room."

"I notice that you have a cellar."

"That's one of the first things I did when we moved onto the homestead—dug the cellar. Quite a few times we've hurried into it when we've seen a funnel-shaped cloud coming."

"It says here you pasture horses and cattle for others."

"That's right. Farmers on irrigated land don't have big pastures. They pay me fifty cents a month per animal to watch their stock during the summer months."

"You report that you have more than twenty acres in crops.

Is the land fenced? Have you been successful with the crops?"

"There is a fence around the 320 acres. The garden and crops are fenced to keep out the animals. This year we had a big garden and also raised potatoes, corn, and feed grains for the animals. The average precipitation in our area is fourteen inches a year. I've been lucky—so far the rains have come at the right time."

"Mr. Adams, I feel you'll continue to be lucky. I notice from Mr. Raymond's report that no one appeared to protest your application. If you will pay a filing fee of ten dollars, the commission of four dollars, and testimonial fees of two and a half dollars, I'll forward your application for a certificate of ownership to the Commissioner of the General Land Office in Washington, D.C. I'll give you a duplicate of this application. It will probably take a year for you to get the certificate of ownership, but be assured you'll receive it."

When the judge finished talking to Papa, he asked the two witnesses to come forward. "You've heard Mr. Adams's testimony," he told them. "Do you say it was correct?"

Both men said, "I do."

The judge rose, shook hands with Papa, and left the room. Papa walked over and took Helen in his arms. As we went down the courthouse steps, he beamed at Mamma and said, "Well, Edna, I guess our moving days are over."

When the certificate of ownership, signed by President Woodrow Wilson, finally arrived, it was dated July 29, 1918.

THE UNITED STATES OF AMERICA

To all to whom these presents shall come, Greeting:

Homestead Certificate No. 641922

Application 017473

Whereas There has been deposited in the GENERAL LAND OFFICE of the United States a CERTIFICATE OF THE REGISTER of THE LAND OFFICE at _Alliance, Nebraska_, whereby it appears that, pursuant to the Act of Congress approved 20th May, 1862, "To secure Homesteads to Actual Settlers on the Public Domain," and the acts supplemental thereto, the claim of _Merlan E. Adams_ has been established and duly consummated, in conformity to law, for the _southeast quarter of section seven, the south half of the southwest quarter of section eight and the east half of the northwest quarter of section seventeen, in township twenty-three north of range fifty-four west of the sixth Principal Meridian, Nebraska, containing three hundred twenty acres;_

according to the OFFICIAL PLAT of the Survey of the said Land, returned to the GENERAL LAND OFFICE by the SURVEYOR GENERAL:

Now know ye, That there is, therefore, granted by the UNITED STATES unto the said _Merlan E. Adams_ the tract of Land above described; **To have and to hold** the said tract of Land, with the appurtenances thereof, unto the said _Merlan E. Adams_ and to _his_ heirs and assigns forever; and there is reserved from the lands hereby granted, a right of way thereon for ditches or canals constructed by the authority of the United States.

In testimony whereof I, _Woodrow Wilson_, PRESIDENT OF THE UNITED STATES OF AMERICA, have caused these letters to be made Patent, and the seal of the GENERAL LAND OFFICE to be hereunto affixed.

GIVEN under my hand, at the CITY OF WASHINGTON, the _29th_ day of _July_, in the year of our Lord one thousand nine hundred _and eighteen_, and of the Independence of the United States the one hundred and _forty third_.

By the PRESIDENT: _Woodrow Wilson_

By. _M. P. LeRoy_

LQ. Lamar, Secretary.

Recorded: _Nebraska_ Vol. _9_, page _176_ _____ Recorder of the General Land Office.

The certificate of ownership for the Adams homestead.

Afterword

THE PRAIRIE SOIL WAS FERTILE. In 1919 Papa sold over one thousand dollars' worth of watermelons from a five-acre patch. He also planted potatoes that were certified for seed. His potatoes won so many blue ribbons at shows in the midwestern states that he acquired the nickname "Spud" Adams. In 1932 Papa was elected to the state legislature at Lincoln as a representative for Scotts Bluff County. In 1940 he was elected president of the Nebraska Growers' Association, and in 1946 he was appointed a federal potato inspector.

For about fifteen years, farmers continued to bring their cattle for pasture each summer. On horseback Howard, Dorothy, Helen, and I herded 150 to 200 head on the unfenced preserve around Lake Alice.

When the drought and the Depression came, my parents sold the homestead and moved to an irrigated farm they had bought in 1927. Papa died a month before their sixty-first wedding anniversary; he was eighty-three. They were devoted and helpful companions to each other for all those years. Mamma lived to be eighty-seven.

Howard skipped two and a half grades before he graduated from high school at sixteen. He attended the University of Nebraska and became a successful civil engineer.

Dorothy was valedictorian of her high school class when she graduated at sixteen. She taught in a rural school for six years before she married a pharmacist.

Helen married a successful farmer. She earned a master's degree in elementary education and has taught school for more than thirty years.

I earned a teacher's certificate when I was eighteen. Over the next fourteen years I taught in five different country schools. I have taught in many parts of the United States and in Germany. I am now retired and live with my husband, John, in California.

T.A.S.